C000104553

MIDNIGHT CAFÉ

MIDNIGHT CAFÉ

SUSANA CUARTAS-ORDOÑEZ

BLACK SPRUCE PRESS

Black Spruce Press
Copyright © 2020 by Susana Cuartas-Ordoñez
All rights reseved.

ISBN 978-1-7338882-6-4

The cover is a photograph titled "Wies in de moriaan" by Dutch
artist Ineke Kamps, used with the kind permission of the artist,
whose work may also be found at www.inekekamps.com

Black Spruce Press / First Book Series
blacksprucepress.org
blacksprucepress@gmail.com
Design by forgetgutenberg.com

Manufactured in the United States of America

CONTENTS

THIS IS FOR YOU

This is for those who've never kissed their mother's knees
for mothers still knowing their child's favorite color
and years from now
kids who still think that color looks best on trees.
For girls who never got crowned a princess
that hid in that corner
made to play that damsel
when they just wanted G.I Joe's with sand in their hands.
For kids who find friends for family
for friends who know you need some family
when four walls can't be called a home anymore.
This is for putting the phone down
having pockets with more than just double taps
for the moments you only live once.
Like that first kiss
those reckless drives
a sunrise worth drinking to
and their last words.
This is in memory for bones close to dust
still growing fire in their breath.
For falling in love like children do
eyes closed
hands open
loving scraped knees
loving broken hearts willing to risk breaking again more.
For poems like Band-Aids to battle scars
for late night coffee and wine
the three a.m. diner conversations
the endlessness of summer
for sunday mornings you actually want to smile about.
To brown girls whose glory has always been turned question
for teachers that actually love teaching
saving future Picassos and Sylvia Plaths from boxed in tests.
To the ones that haven't made it yet
walking in cities that don't know your name

and ones that know it well.
Stealing sunsets in Harlem
finding beauty in brokenness
this is to what a real man is
finding his pride in all the right places.
For the generation with the lost tongue
for the ones that have been doing something about it
leaving some bones to shake
praying to a God they think doesn't love them.
Go on,
find the real God in you
This.
This is for you.
To remind you that you're worth something
that life is never meant to settle easily
there is beauty in that too
that most days
I am trying to make something worthy with these hands.
So walk with me,
through the corridors of this thing we call a heart.
Let's try to make sense of it all

NEW YORK CITY LOVER

Welcome to New York City,
the unofficial foster home for hopeless romantics
mourning lost unrequited lovers.
You'll find them in coffee shops, the kind open till two a.m.
tongues coated in loneliness and nostalgia,
joking amongst themselves about how life would be
if they never fell in love.
I'll be among them
drinking coffee filled with melancholy, reminding me
of the aftertaste her lips left on me.
I'll tell them,
I've got a stutter with her name
her laugh still echoes in the crook of my neck
while my bedsheets are starting to ask questions.
Why doesn't she come around anymore?
was this never home for her then?
I went searching for answers not long ago
found her walk in Queens
the closest thing to her talk in Midtown
bumped into her smile on the boardwalk
used it as a point of reference to catch my breath.
That night,
I spilled my sins over the Brooklyn bridge
said my prayers to the city skyline.
In hopes to find some kind of god in me
while she's been the devil to my insides
that I've been holding like an ideology.
Now, my ribcage is grinding its bones to dust
excavating all the bits and pieces of her
there is a turmoil you find living inside yourself
for those
who will never love you back.
So you'll find me there,
on that Harlem rooftop
getting drunk off cheap corner store wine

with tatttered pages of Pablo Neruda whispering
"Me gustas cuando callas"
The only lovers of mine that I know to find a morning after
so this city,
full of malice and glory.
Wraps me in its arms to find solace in the sidewalk cracks
where I spill her out in ink
that children will play hopscotch on, in memory of us
so that at least somewhere
under this New York City skyline
We.
Still exist together.

BEING HONEST FOR ONCE

I've got my father's sadness and my mother's pride
I'm the cataclysmic aftermath
that results when two lonely hearts clash.
Momma doesn't ask me if I pray anymore
guess it's because she's realized me and god
had some falling out of sorts.
I don't wear a cross on my neck anymore
because the one on my back is enough for me to carry.
To be honest,
nobody knows I met God for the first time in a girl's smile
how I love like my father and my mother.
I love too deeply, and I love too long
catch myself loving all the wrong ones
fell in love only once so far
Got her stuck in between my teeth now
picking out parts of her from my smile
finding the ghost of her in any cigarette that I happen to smoke.
You can hear her skeleton knocking from my bedroom closet
some nights
never told her
she was my favorite sunday morning
I can't remember how many there were.
Now,
all I've got to show
is a ribcage for a graffiti wall
from all the times she's left.
So, I apologize, to those who will love me after this
for they will have a hard time building a home here
amongst all this wreckage
But yeah,
I'm a young kid
merely twenty years on this earth
still
I've got an old soul with stories to write from my laugh lines.
Never minding the ink I spill whenever I bleed

with a shotgun for a tongue looking like a graveyard full of stars.
Everyone says I've got a nice smile
still trying to figure out how this smile actually works
and my hands?
They're like my father's smooth and calloused
because I'm still learning how to hold things correctly
whenever I hold something
my palms get sweaty
to remind me just how easy you can lose things.
Ask me what I'm afraid of?
There will be very little
but I am afraid of this,
I'm afraid I'll never fall in love like "that" again
I'm afraid I'll become just like my father
more than his hands.
That all the skeletons in my closet will come out again
they're the kind that like playing with my demons in the dark
hoping my shadow won't be ashamed of all it bears witness to.
To be honest,
I'm quieter than I should be
my voice is merely a whisper or nothing at all
but give me some paper and a pen.
I'll show you what a two-a.m. confessional looks like.
I love in a way I've yet to fully understand
don't think I ever will.
I've got a crooked smile from all the times it's been broken,
a ribcage too small to tame this heart,
I don't mind being alone, but I do hate the lonely
that's why coffee shops and strangers
are my most familiar friends.
In the end, there are some days I'm struggling to breathe
with lungs filled to the brim in my own darkness
an ashtray at the bottom of my stomach
holding everything I want to forget.
I'm a collection of all the chaos you can find in a sinner
that's going to sin again.
An unconventional soul who calls herself a poet

writing love letters folded into paper airplanes on rooftops
surrounded by half empty wine bottles,
all the melancholy these hands can carry,
and Nina Simone in the background.

LETTER TO YOURSELF #1

Dear you,
you've started hearing the echoes of past sins
the kind that leave a smudge the more you try to get rid of it.
The collection of post-it notes in your pocket continue to swell
you are twenty.
Lost, a tremble in your voice, no real place to feel at home.
Do not resent him too long for not coming to your graduation
in some years, he will be an ocean away.
The moment you tell him goodbye will be fleeting
the father you once knew withered away through time.
Know that you will still have so much left to say
caught
like summer fireflies inside the mason jar of your throat
each one a wish left unmade
remember what he taught.
That it is just for a moment
that this too shall come and go
all of it.
Simply another moment for the angels to gossip about.

J COLE'S ALBUM DROP

J Cole dropped Forest Hills during the coldest winter of my life
it was the kind of cold that left your feet stuck
frozen to the floor
in a car
at three a.m.
talking about things you didn't want the sun to shine on.
On a night once lived that knew no bounds
that tasted bold and reeked of forgiveness
for the morning's truth to find.
Of the bitter darkness that took the God out of you
and you've been trying to find your way back to it ever since
or something worth believing in at least.
I'm sometimes something hard to love.
Stitched up in places that make me believe
Picasso likes to come out some nights
and have his way with my heart.
How many signatures do you think he can fit into this spine?
How many secrets can you say your chest actually carries?
Since twelve, I've known how bitter secrets can be
I haven't stopped counting since.
The reasons,
for my father's shadow
my mother's lonely
why some words just aren't meant for you.
Like stay here.
Stay now.
Stay always.
Some days I wonder what's worse
never being chosen
or never being asked to choose in the first place?
Just take what you get,
and roll with it.
Or roll it up, smoke it in and drown it out.
Remember that somewhere,
someone wants to love the loneliness out of your smile

the brokenness in your hands
stitched up, misshapen heart and all.
Have a thunder that calms that tiresome storm inside your chest.
Remind yourself, that just because you love someone,
doesn't mean they have the right to claim you without permission
suck the marrow from your bones
make a mess out of your holy.
Instead,
find it somewhere to collect dust
the notes tucked underneath the bed somewhere.
A proper way to prove our existence
not together
just side by side made up of things not quite meant to last.
The moments I'll tell my daughter about
when her heart whispers to her for the first time
in ways that'll make her feel heavy.
And me?
I'll know all too well.
Of the smile,
that created Greek glories and tragedies all at the same time.
Become just stories of an old fall
some ancient youth.

CONVERSATIONS FOR THE WITCHING HOUR

We found ourselves at a coffee shop one night
wine in our bellies and truths in our mouths.
The cards of our hearts laid out onto a wooden table like psalms
answers to a prayer.
You carried the queen of hearts, me the ace of spades.
Stacks laid among us by the end of the witching hour
of all the contemplations ever made
love was not meant to be easy
this time
now
or ever.
By the end of it all,
when the clock strikes whatever time has been chosen
ending just another moment.
No place called home will be found with you in it.
Love is not the fairytale your mother told you about
maybe I should carry the joker in my back-pocket instead
maybe I should start calling it Russian roulette
maybe this is the last time I'll spin the chamber.
Love is not meant to be understood,
saints go out in full moons to dance with sinners by morning,
you can't tell the difference between the two.
There is no winner this time around
whoever looks at this hand
will know how much has been lost
and tried to be found again
so cheers,
to everything we were and weren't
maybe we'll get it right next round.

MEMOIR OF A LOVER

I've tried to write you out of me more times
than I can count with both hands
for two years
I've yet to find that poem inside me
or at the bottom of this pen.

So how about we call this the will dedicated to my sins?
I wrote your name on another woman's flesh last night
it's not the first time either.
I've got it stitched to the roof of my tongue
I'm surprised she didn't ask about you
how you could leave so much chaos in this body.
Truth is,
I'm trying to piece myself back together again
with things that don't exist in your name.
Been told it takes seven months to shed the first layer of skin
it's been more than seven
a year has passed since the last time we kissed.
I can still find you there sometimes
in parts of my hands like wine stains on carpet
as if to say I will be able to find you always now.

If they ever ask about it all I'll tell them
she's the kind of girl that'd stand on train tracks
just so she could say
she's felt the earth tremble beneath her feet.
She has a devilish smile
ocean for eyes, the kind you'd gladly drown in
and a laugh that always sounds wholesome.
You smiled and God made a little more sense
tasting of bad intentions, the first time we kissed.
Learned that lust drips down like honey
for those who have snuck into each other's dreams before.

I'll be honest here,
I never said much.
Momma found out I fell in love just hearing me say your name
wish I'd told her then
momma she can sing.
Her voice carries all my favorite songs now
with no way to make them mine.
Constellations having carried witness to it all
a reminder,
in all this sea of mess
love laid here too some moons ago.
Something holy made in between sinners
how recklessly we crashed into one another
you bruised a little
I chipped a tooth.
The first time I felt beautiful our lips were covered in red wine
your eyes told me I was beautiful
more than your hands.

That night you tucked away the instruction manual to my heart
I've yet to get it back.
Falling in love with you
felt like an alcoholic cliff diving off of sobriety
truth is
I loved you more than I'd like to admit to
think of you more times than I should
hope for things I shouldn't
that in the end I'll never get.
New York doesn't seem like magic anymore,
she is a lonely city now, a quiet lover.
I thought you'd leave everything as you first found it
you didn't.
I'm here now with just the phantom of you
the ghost of a memory caressing the lonely of my own shadow.
Accompanied by a mason jar of questions inside my throat
that hold no answers.

FRANK'S INTERLUDE

Frank Ocean isn't saying the same things anymore
neither are we.
The recklessness in your bones stopped whispering to you.
I don't carry around a pack of sins to smoke
my chest is much quieter now, your conscience must weigh less
I wonder what your mother must think of all this.
Have you cried to her about me?
Mourned me out in smoke yet?
How often have you said my name?
What kind of ghost am I to you?
What story do your hands tell about us?
My hands have been witness,
some hearts can only be kissed once.
After being left wrung out,
from giving all they could.
A decade of history written out in three years of flesh
we've stopped searching for our love poems
let the hourglass run dry
tucked it somewhere
in between the breath of a distant yesterday
and some other life that is not mine.
Frank didn't tell us we were going to end up like this.

ANSWERS AT TWENTY-ONE

Answers found at twenty-one
November is a bitter beast to hold,
where the truth hides in the light
and the dark tells it, boldly.
My vice for recklessness just lingers in a late-night drive
on a midnight hour.
New York is a lost home that I don't hang around much anymore
my heart now
is a messy thing to handle at times.
Having left it in hands that were not so careful with me.
Guess that's why you'll never find stunt doubles around,
always looked like you were having a war with yourself
and me in the crossfire
white flag in hand, set to watch.
By the time the smoke cleared, you already left
never caring to look back those days.
Nowadays,
I'm holding something more than a white flag
more than the mishaps of coming from a broken marriage,
with an already too broken heart,
and another poem to write about it.
Because I still scar easy
have a mess of ink often
constructing a road map from what I've learned of my heart
so far.
The silence in my father still lingers to him
as if it's the only lover he's ever stayed loyal to
I've still yet to write out his silence.
Or the nostalgia that comes with the memory
that he too once had a smile
I don't know where he's left it.
I wonder if he remembers now.
His reality and mine are worlds away from one another
but we can still drink wine from the same mason jar somewhere.

So far at twenty-one,
I'm more like my mother than I give credit to
like my father in ways I don't care to admit to.
Don't know what that forever type of love looks like
but I've read scripture in her skin.
That love is not all that bitter,
to be broken does not always mean to be loved.
Mangos with lime and salt were the best excuse to run barefoot,
when bruised kneecaps was the most dangerous event you could
fathom
I still haven't walked Paris barefoot, or Rome
they might have to wait awhile.
Instead,
I have my father's lessons and my mother's prayers
conversations that keep me honest
countless of unfinished poems trying to prove it
with a heart that's still learning the worth of its own heartbeat.

TALES OF SUMMER

Whenever you'd put the top down
meant summer had come around.
This time,
carrying the melancholy of our last kiss in the passenger side
reminisced over a bar table
to prove time had its fill of us.
With our youth at its peak
easiest to bruise,
the courage you needed nowhere to be found.
Unable to put the pieces together, that portrait still stays empty.
My heart stumbles across your memory some nights
over the witching hour
letting our sins whisper out each other's names
if only just for a night.
When the moon got bitter for the both of us
knowing about all the truths we've spilled
just to do nothing with by morning.
Where do you hide them to make sure they don't make noise?
Where they don't jog your memory that this too mattered
I've always wondered what it tasted like to you in the first place.
But hey, everyone's got something to teach someone.
If I came back, I wonder if you'd ask what took you so long?
Like a season you came and left
a glory of all four together
full intention of simply passing on through
bringing along its own mourning
because everyone knows.
The same season never happens twice

HEARTBEAT

The heartbreak that got cradled in my back pocket
is underneath the bed now
well, most of it.
The rest got penned out
gets talked about whenever we break bread
you'll find, that God's angels too get curious.
They'll wonder if that's all there is to it?
It is.
Her apologies
are stacked neatly in between Neruda and Bukowski.
I can be found in the bottom left corner of her library.
The eulogies of this life and all the ones before
fill up the dashboard next to the poems I never cared about.
My cousin's name is balled up in there somewhere
still have yet to swallow that death whole
still have yet to swallow this holy in its entirety.
I carry all my mother's lessons in my gut
it's the only place I know that will listen to them well enough.
Anywhere else has a scar to show
for why it wasn't meant to be there to begin with.
Time
gave me permission to tuck all the lies that my father sugarcoats
underneath its hands.
Did the math of how many years he hopes to last doing
whatever it is that's made him run from us for so long.
Said that three of those years will be spent sleeping
In the end,
he hopes to find a weeping willow to be buried under.
The reminder,
you are only here for however long your lungs decide to keep on
breathing.
When they stop for a second,
when mind and body disconnect
the chest caves in
No matter what
I have to remind it
Work.

LETTER TO YOURSELF #2

Dear you,
You are twenty-two and foolish still
lost in a maze of your own darkness
along the way you bump into her
a break in time
a caught breath
a jump in the past come anew, bold, and everlasting
tender hands
the birth of her creations starts here.
One morning, before the sun had woken
she grew a bouquet of flowers out your spine
it was the first time anyone ever made you magic.
Still having so much to learn
not knowing of the gold you hold in your hands
for so long, you will not be willing to understand
to always bare your teeth does not make one the strongest.

LETTER TO MY FUTURE DAUGHTER

Dear baby girl,
When you find yourself searching for the right foundation
to stand upon in becoming a woman.
Do not think of me,
but think of your grandmother.
For I am simply a fragment of her in its entirety
your grandmother crossed the border at twenty-two years old.
Three days before leaving,
told her parents they weren't her home anymore.
Instead, carried them and a country once hers
in the pockets of a yellow jumpsuit.
Crossed a river that had more holy than holy water,
filled in an abundance of prayers and rosaries swallowed whole.
Running,
because she's got "la migra" stuck at her heels
and doesn't look back often
look back on that one night she had to bust out the window
from a man who wanted more than just her money.
Ask your own mother of pain
she'll show you the depths of a woman's sorrows.
I know people often say
that sometimes a woman
can be as strong as a man
I like to think certain men are just man enough
to handle all the goddess in women.
Your grandfather only lasted seventeen years,
your grandmother has yet to regret that since.
Baby girl,
we often entrust ourselves to people
who have yet learned the use of their own hands.

So,
when you find yourself with someone that has unglorified you
remind yourself of her, and how she with all her fury
like when Eve pulled herself out of Adam's ribcage.

Proved she was always whole to begin with,
made sure to be loved correctly.
No little boy that opens doors and smiles nice,
but a man with steady hands and whose knees don't buckle
when he sees a woman with two kids.
You carry the living bibliography of a woman
that people will wonder about, when they see the fire in you.
Tell them.
Your DNA holds the matriarchy of a woman
that has an accent hidden in between her teeth
there is a glory in her veins that tells you
"rest here I'll carry the weight with you"
has got drums for a heartbeat to the voice of
Hector Lavoe and Willie Colon.
A steel rod for a spine
ready to defend
all she's worked for
all she's been standing for
all she's been fighting for.
Her favorite saying hidden in the curve of her cheeks
the one I hope you'll come to learn it's worth as well
"no hay nada malo en soñar grande"
Ain't nothing wrong with dreaming big baby
Ain't nothing wrong with dreaming big.

COFFEE TALK

Our most honest conversation
happened on an odd night over shared wine
when I was a visitor where not much belonged to me
not even you.
I had your last name, alongside your walk
didn't finish the bottle, we didn't need to
didn't need much for the bough to break.

Enter into the library of my father's ribcage
for what seems like the first time
found the stacks of books he carries.
Stories he talks about but never actually tells.
Like the drunk walks to his father's grave
running out by morning
laid beside the rest of whatever lessons
he's been waiting to put on display for me
part boy and part flaw these create the bearings of my father's heart.

You cried that night,
I'm not apologizing for it either.
It's true, that most men need it too
more times than this world or themselves have allowed
I think you need it most still.
Tell me, have you cried since?
Do you believe the prayers you say every other sunday?

You do well not to cling on a memory that's not today
when the trees do not settle for you
I hope you never forget,
the weight your name carries inside your mother's throat.
There is no love story here you say
if there is how small of a box does it fit in?
Only today is of worth to you to hell with the rest of it right?
You only hope for breath till ninety-nine

that way
there's no chance for celebrating reaching a century.
Holding stories in hands made of mountains and books
so far, this is what I call the definition of a simple man at heart.

STATUS HISTORY

My mother no longer understands this country's voice
she's never heard it sound this way before.
How it tries to
whiteout our names
whitewash our cultures
make a mockery of this skin we live in.
I know rejection for having makings of a foreign tongue
when I talk.
By the sixth grade down in the south somewhere
I got told I don't belong here to begin with.
To go back where I came from.
That this is America, so speak english around here.
Funny these days I can't help but notice
whose taking care of the children in Beverly hills?
White boys behind white picket fences
don't get taught to call the food they throw on their white floors
privilege.
According to the US census bureau by 2020
43 million will be speaking this language.
In the meantime, news nowadays propagates
we should be thankful they don't kick us out.
That they'd be better off without our kind.
That us cockroaches have done nothing to deserve this land
Except for...
Bernardo de Galvez.
He helped Washington get your freedom.
500,000 of us fought beside you in World War two
when we weren't even being considered a category back then.
Men like Marcario Garcia who carried a medal of honor
yet still you didn't let him sit at your table.
As if it has ever been a right you conquered fairly.
There's a reason why the earth is the color that it is
why things grow through concrete
and coals make diamonds under pressure.
Come to learn that the purest things usually got some dirt on it

we've bloodied and paid enough debts with hands to know.
Just look at what's been built upon this land you call yours
even the fruit on your kitchen table
is ours
before you swipe something for it.
You will never understand our stories
you have yet been willing to listen.
My father's accent is a reminder...
The south doesn't always taste likes peaches
children with silver spoons
do not know the need of having to fit into outgrown shoes.
What it is to feed a family that knows hunger
all too well, for all too long.
Children
who only have voices for parents
through cellphones and Facebook posts.
So, so what if my full name doesn't fit into your excel sheet?
My parents' skin is a testimony
their worth is more than any degree could ever offer.
Do not try to straighten out what is meant to unfurl like whiplash
I come from empty pockets who crossed borders
and broke their backs to fill for me to stand on.
You learn how to do that when you come from fire
the breath in their lungs is all the homeland I'll ever need.
Realize,
you can learn from us
our blood has become accustomed
in always having to do more than necessary
just to get what's rightfully ours.

CONVERSATIONS WITH GOD

I wonder what it would be like to talk to god one day
find him on a park bench drinking coffee or tea
whichever one he likes best.
Ask him, what's your favorite color?
Are the stars your best friends that keep you company?
How do you turn things into existence?
Can you rub your fingers together to create galaxies?
Is the boom in thunder your laughter when you can't contain it?
Can you help me the decipher the anatomy of a prayer?
Or the anatomy of a woman?

The hail Mary's in my tongue are simply phantoms now
after they told me "god won't ever want you"
that I'm something more devil than god
that there's no god left for me at all
you see why church pews never meant much for my knees?

They heard somewhere along the way
that two daughters of Eve loving one another
is a savage thing.
Worse, than the married man whose silhouette
hides the battle scars he painted onto his wife last night
A woman's lipstick,
carries all the remnants of men she's left behind in hotel beds
while at home
they're waiting for her to come back from another
"late night shift"
They say you'll find that all true believers
carry whips for rosaries and scorebooks for bibles
making the loudest noise
in hopes
that the good old days still exist to those pearly gates
all the while when the church bells start ringing
look at how they stop praying
rushing out like children do for recess.

Talking about the newly single mother's slightly wrinkled dress
when she was too busy actually taking care of her children
Instead
I found you in ungodly places
in a drug addicted prayer for forgiveness
in those who tend to be in the devil's playground for too long
in every mother's plea of innocence for children of some darker skin.
This is where I found God
not tucked away in church bells
I found you in peculiar places.
In my mother's dusted up wedding ring
in my father's brokenness
in this pen
and these hands.
I got my palms read one night
wondering if they were touching all the right things
if you're jealous of us
because we too mortals are able to feel like gods in this life
sometimes
is this why you gave us loneliness?

But until then
until I can ask whether you like Paris or Rome better
when they call me a sinner
the devil's favorite play thing
that there is no place for me in heaven.
Remember
I'm not just malice and sin
I've got calloused hands covered in ink
with all the strength my parents taught me to survive this world
in my pocket.
Writing down poems from the broken parts of me
if white gates truly are not meant for me
that's ok.
Simply point me to where the old romantics lay to nap
for what does it matter if I am no longer there to make it whole?
There are better things to worry about.

I want to walk cobble stone covered streets the whole night
watch the sunrise in Kigali, Rome, Cairo, and Paris
gift my mother a home and my father his smile
see if I can figure out why we love love
but can't fall in it
someday find the divine in silence.
So yeah, I'm a sinner
that likes rooftop conversations listening to the hum of angels
a woman's smile next to me the morning after.
So when they ask how can I believe in God?
I'll tell them.
Since when did God ever pick favorites?

MIDNIGHT VICES

Sunday mornings don't exist for her
you'll never get a sunrise that's kissed her skin
but ask the shadows they suit her better.
Cling
as if they're the only things she's ever stayed faithful to
makes sure she's never alone at night
so the ghosts won't haunt her.
Most nights fuse together into one; especially the weekends.
With the devil sewn into her insides
shows it out in that little black dress
perfume spelling out lust
stained red lipstick
holding all the names she's ever laid in bed with.
Stiletto heels that fit the description
of a wolf dressed in sheep's wool like a wanted sign—
tempt all the men and women in the room.
Sends them to recheck their makeup
they'll soon find out
she doesn't need a bass drop to grab attention.
Just have her hips do a swing or two
cross her legs like a lady
smile like she knows some things, ready to go to work.
Sinners have the tendency to trade some sins for her time
she'll know how to lick the God out of your tongue
burn the holy from your bones
claw at your insides
hands behind her back.
Give you a confessional that doesn't task prayers for penance
you get an unmade bed cloaked in late night vices.
By morning she's no longer there
left alone
awakened
to the ghost of her on your lips
a note on your skin saying.
She's the real reason why Eve ate the apple in the first place.

LONELY HOUR

One day
if you wander around corners during the lonely hour of a city.
You'll find,
for saints
there is no place here to call home.
For sinner's
a sunrise is always too high a price to pay.
Deep in the red hook
you can hear the clashing wars of wine and spirits.
We are infidels released from purgatory in clouds of smoke
those nights, the moon hung low to her skirt
kissed at her ankles.
Sang a song that held a thousand tears
for you,
for me,
for how deep the depth of scars really go.
Echoing along desolate brick wall
while you stain your hands from red to black and blue
till they do your bidding.
How much time has passed since then?
What luck can you find in the pocket of a beggar?
What tragedy can be told from the crown of a king?
What love can you spare to both?
Like the blind do for their eyes
like the wicked do for their kin
like I did for you.

LIST OF BOTTLES

I've yet to find a bottle that explains my father's tragedy
one that tastes like my mother's sadness
my father's smile no longer exists.
I've yet to find the bottle that tastes of my own broken
I looked through all New York
trying to find something that tasted like our last kiss
I didn't bother trying to find our first.
Went to all the coffee shops you might've liked
stopped in Harlem.
Found the station that gave you a sunset worth remembering
maybe because I got you to love this city once more
maybe because I was there too.
I got the taste of a reckless night
catching a rooftop high somewhere on Lexington and East 42nd.
After having some jack for courage
the kind I could never find for you.
Maybe once
or twice
when the morning was nowhere in sight
though the night had already done its deed
smoke lingered as the only excuse to hold onto the moment.
Did you know a cigarette could taste like too late?
Always too late.
I got stuck counting for you
with all the time I found in my pockets
counting the seconds, minutes, hours of my own lonely
echoing through for company.
It's why some nights I let you in when the angels fall asleep.

THE MAKE-UP OF A BROKEN HEART

When they ask me what makes up a broken heart?
I'll simply say your name
show them my hands
tell them of all the stories there are
where I went so far left for you
always got caught jumping off the cliff
and you
nowhere to be found to save me.
Say
I loved her with such a fury, made me grow out of my silence
showed me just how pretty my words could be.
These are the moments that are meant for you to fall in love
then break you.

For a while I clung to your memory
getting high off it while it was still fresh
reeking of everything you think you once wanted one day
overdosed on you too much
way too quick.
Paying it off with the nickels, dimes, and pennies
you left in my pocket from the night before.
Nowadays, ghosts sometimes share their lonely with me
you are thin in between my fingertips
The ghost of you likes to come with the cold often
maybe to lend me the jacket I left in your closet a year ago.
Maybe to remind me of a life we all once lived
the life of you only faint.

In the middle of a cigarette
of a shot glass
of anything you can deal to your demons for a night off
or maybe just an hour or so for a quick rendezvous at least
anything to live another life that isn't one of a lonely poet.
These are the types of things you learn
that make lovers
the most dangerous addictions for broken hearts.

DAYDREAMS & DAISIES

Momma dreamt me up in a yellow sundress and daisies
laid a crown of them on my head.
I think she painted me white there.
With hopes I'd get something better than a ring
carrying a memoirs worth of old secrets.
She pawned it off in exchange for a chain of ghosts
I wonder if she tells them secrets too.
At some point,
my skin started craving darker shades
so, when I shaded myself blue
she started dreaming me yellow.
Now,
I've got a fistful of daisies for the girl next door.
She's stopped dreaming in yellow
and prayed me in white
with a bag full of crowns trailing behind.
She must still hope for the little girl with daisies in her hair
or the yellow sundress.
Because I stopped liking yellow
while the dress?
Is lost somewhere.
And the daisies?
Well, I've got them in another girl's hair
I'll share them with you if you'd like.
I've got an album box full of the ones they've left behind
we can trade what haunts us over tea one day if you'd like.
When the box is full
the chains been broken
Did you know I pawned off their laughter?
For more than a couple of hits?
How many times I've had to color back in a broken heart?
Will I hear the echoes of your first love?
How do you take your heartache?
Dark but sweet?
Light and bitter?

By this time,
I don't think they ever cared much for daisies
the same way I never cared for yellow.
Although, I'll tell you of the one who left the daisies in her hair
because she liked how they looked with her yellow sundress
while listening to my daydreams.
Momma can you paint her in white?

SANDCASTLES

Build a sandcastle with me
collect a seashell that the ocean's whispered her name into
keep it a secret.
I'll learn to play piano;
maybe one day we'll find ourselves at a bar
you'll smile for me one last time
perhaps I can leave first?
Back when we were young, reckless, thinking love was easy.
The secret life we found ourselves in
are decades past and lonesome.
The cherry blossoms are blooming now
the table we used to sit at bare
no more wine left to drink,
coffee to brew,
things to spill.
They can find a street corner dedicated to you
in every city I've ever been to
a couple of regrets that follow close behind
sometimes a bottle too to forget.
A concept I now deem,
remembering something you never knew to begin with.
I can coax out every time we kissed off the ends of moonlight.
I'm now the book always kept in your shelf
picked up from the basement of an antique shop
paid with the careless change you happen to have in your pocket.
End up being the kind of book
meant to only fill up empty spaces
never meant to be missed.
I'm still on your shelf,
waiting,
streetlights flickering away
as the ghosts resurrect themselves again every sunset.

BLUEPRINT OF A MAN

I'm mapping out the blueprint of a man through my father's silence
there's a raging storm inside his chest
made him lose his voice somewhere, for a while now.
My father has calloused hands
stained at nine years old with his father's eulogy
that's why he learned to sleep with ghosts.
Were you able to grasp enough of him to hold onto even now?
How thin is it?
Do you remember his voice?
Have you clung to his laughter?
Do you have his smile?
Or is his memory another ghost you sleep with to meet again?

My father stands as tall as a church
the makeup for a silent man
he's got a sea glass collection for a heart
makes all his sins look pretty.
Has something of a voice
between pages of Marquez and Dostoevsky
I wonder,
did their words coax out your secrets onto their pages?
How many of them are drowned in wine?
How many bottles have become confessionals?
I know I'm one of them
How many sheets have you left unsettled?
How long is your rap sheet?
Were you the type to leave in the middle of the night?
With nothing of a trace for the morning to find
Which of them looked like my mother?
Which of them did you tell them my name?
Were you the type to hide the ring in your pocket?
Did you even wear it at all on those nights?
Is this what you tried to brush away?

A castle of bottles building underneath your bed,
ready to break, under the last roof we shared together.
What home does your heart carry now?
Do you know,
I have your walk; my eyes can carry as many stories as you
a heart that's been loved but left plenty.
They say I talk like you too
I tell them,
of the man who gifted me his love for books
and all the lessons he carries hidden in his wallet
Did you know,
I chased after you on my bike one morning.
You still had your smile back then,
I have not found that man since.

LETTER TO YOURSELF #3

Dear you,
Now twenty-three,
in a world your parents told you so often about
you did not heed their warnings well enough.
Letting the fear of your father's shadow linger for too long
your footsteps are starting to look like his
your heart has broken enough times
be gentle with it now.
Knowing thousands of moments that are still left undone
do not lose yourself in the mix of all the noise
do not let this silence linger for too long
there is a reason for it to have been this way.
Do not repeat the failed cycle others have done before you
if you must, fail in a new way then.
Tenacity was in you once
find it again.
These moments,
are yours for the taking
if not now, when?
Remember,
you have lost and found yourself again through worse.

WRITE WHAT YOU KNOW

They told me write what you know.
Well,
I know of heartbreak
I know love like a jawbreaker that makes your teeth hurt
makes you wonder what's so sweet about it
that everyone keeps talking about
asking where you can go find it.
When all you've gotten to hold
is a copper field inside your mouth.
I know falling in love whole
being loved out of to pieces.
Kept company by nights that got us
drunk, high and everything else that can't be called holy
after midnight
strung together by misfortunes.
The kind of ghosts' people should fear most
are ones that aren't afraid of appearing in bare morning.
While some time ago,
our bodies made deals with one another
that we don't know about.
I'm a romantic with a side of masochist to come along with it.
Melancholy,
tastes like the last kiss that you didn't know would be the last
lived out till its final lingering second.
You'll learn that sometimes,
all the people you've ever loved could be strangers to you now.
Are they?

SOMEDAY, SOMEWHERE, SOMEHOW

Someday, somewhere, somehow,
someone is getting on a plane
leaving everything behind, including her.
Someday, somewhere, somehow,
someone is mourning.
The sky has never looked so bitter
never looked so lonesome amongst all its splendor
all that can be offered as sacrifice are simple tears
for in spite of it all
this moment here
mattered enough to be proven into existence.
Even if got caught in between time and is lost forever now
some things are not meant to be found
others not meant to be remembered.
Maybe this is one of those moments too?
See this bottle doesn't do it anymore but I still drink it
fill my mouth with aged grapes
from the fisherman's town off the coast of Sicily
let it draw out the corners of my mouth.
I let them know,
I'm just trying to lose some things.
All these proclivities that someday, somewhere, somehow
have left me anything but whole.
All these ghosts
have the essence of old women
knowing all the children in the neighborhood
who still play after the lights come on in Bleecker street.
Their names will be called for
be told of their longing
you are still waiting outside to hear your name be called home.
Is there still ink left?
If so, when will you stop writing her out?
for all the honeycombs you've yet to dip your fingers into
for all those sunsets you haven't talked about
for all the riddles whose spine you have yet to scale

someday, my father's shadow will leave me
somewhere, I'm your first, second, third choice
somehow, my heart will figure itself out
someday,
somewhere.

TO MY MOTHER

Momma fell in love with a southern boy once
swept her off her feet in more ways than my father ever could,
gave her the courage to find the woman she'd hung deep in her
closet
covered in more dust and remember when's than she cared to admit to.
Lace like tangled in between
family obligations
and
no such thing as divorce.

She lost that southern boy years ago, the south along with him,
he had a new home to go to last time she went down there.
And momma, hasn't loved another man like that since.
Instead, she grew out a new smile and a steel spine
holding two daughters up.
She has not let go yet.
While I'm still trying to accept my own apology
for why she left him
to come after me.
Most days,
I'll carry the shame of the first heart I broke being hers.
I've never questioned her love since.

My mother is a collection of a country an ocean away,
of ghosts and what if's and a smile that says
you will never see her fear.
I am an abundance of old love poems, her lessons,
my father's shadow
and remnants of what it's still considered to be whole.

I wonder, does she think of him when her spine isn't all steel?
If she reminds herself as night that she no longer has parents?
If the taste it leaves in her mouth still feels foreign?
I forget sometimes,
how often she has to hold herself whole for appearances.

For herself,
for when she got to the room too late,
a baby gone too quick,
and a marriage that lasted too long.
For me,
when she sees her daughter broken from the weight of a world
that doesn't think too kindly of her.
But holds me up,
talks, like she's got the winning lottery number in her throat
like there's gold in another sunrise
like God got a plan and she's got the inside scoop.
To my mother,
whose blessings everyday remind me that God does exist
I hope on a golden sunrise I can call her up to say
Rest now momma
I got you from here.

THE POET AND ARTIST

Sit with me a while
grab some coffee or tea
sit with me until we are no longer consumed by our own names
until all I know is yours.
I can give you my hands
show that they too carry battle scars
having fought out of my father's shadow
show my heart has all its teeth still
chewing through the remnants of old lovers.
See how much this skin can last?
Maybe by now, I'll have the right type of courage
to withstand opening the gates
of whatever forest you carry in your eyes
maybe by now,
you won't be afraid of loving me
I won't be afraid of love.
So, I'll drink coffee
you'll drink tea
I'll write you this poem on a napkin
for all these words are yours
perhaps you'll draw me a picture.
The poet and the artist,
perhaps our paths in this life
will cross as many times as we've done all our past lives.
For all the ways this world has conspired with us
is nothing short from kissing fate.

ANSWERS FOUND AT TWENTY-FOUR

I'm twenty-four and still writing about love.
This heart echoes at night sometimes
retracing the steps of all the women that have left me
I wonder what to make of it.
I've learned that the heart is just a collection of stretch marks
no matter how many times they leave you
they cannot break you in your entirety.
Even, if you leave the door unlocked
for their ghosts to come in for a visit.
Even, if you haunt yourself to sleep
over all the reasons why they left.
You did well to learn the inside of your heart
and how heavy it can be
so heavy,
you no longer find yourself scaling rooftops—
but you still hide in a city.
Even if it may not be Paris,
there are still cobblestone streets to find
where no one knows your name
where you become a stranger
even to yourself.
Maybe in search of her again
standing somewhere on a sidewalk smiling
or maybe to avoid her altogether just for a moment.
You still tell people you have hands that look like your father's
but they are yours.
Now,
you leave his shadow in your back pocket
to use as a roadmap to find his voice whenever he calls
no longer in search for an apology.
Simply remnants of the man
that held your tears when you cried about love for the first time.
Told you,
"Do not hold onto something in fear of never finding it again."
Having that been said,

I can count the number of times I've fallen in love
with one hand.
Melancholy,
is the only word I've learned without using a dictionary
I carry ink for chapters to this lifespan
each one a story to tell.
About the lost girl,
who found her spine writing some poems
about a lost lover,
one you once loved, learned to love right, never meant to keep
about your mother,
who does not ask for the stories.
Simply puts the pieces back together again
like a makeshift jigsaw puzzle.
In hopes,
that you find that sunday afternoon kind of love
that God make a little more sense
and that maybe, just maybe.
You'll get it right this time around
or at least, another story worth writing about.

GROWING PAINS

Someday, you'll read books with no pictures
cry a song that no one knows the words to
including you.
None that you want to praise in
the definition of praise will get lost somewhere
when you walk down a block and mercy
won't know its way back to you.
But in New York,
a cigarette is always lit.
Someday a bed will become a complicated chaos of a thing
sheets knowing how to carry history now.
When she calls at three a.m.
bed cold and you're the closest warmth willing to come around.
There are no more sweaters left in my closet
that don't carry us somewhere
living some other life from some other time
in between the stitching.
But,
melancholy does well to suffocate the nostalgia out of these sort of things
Someday they will text you from their lonely and you will not answer...
Someday they will text you from their lonely and you will not answer..
Someday they will text you from their lonely and you will not answer.
On the third day, I will be free of her.
To what God will you pray to then?
After that,
you'll allow yourself the luxury to think of her
only when you're drunk enough.
For times like these,
your sins are all you have left to bargain with.
Which isn't often,
to remember
to forget
to remake memories in favor of our own bidding
to survive another day.

TRAIN TRACKS

He called her, on the phone while she sat in a coffee shop,
surrounded by words with nowhere to put them. Asked the kind
of questions you require a lifetime on your hands to answer, and
he offered some explanations. Words aged like brandy and plums
surrounded by the weeping willow branches he plans to be buried
under. Ones that he probably used for himself late at night when
the conscience got full quicker than the wine glass could keep
up with. His world of train tracks. Described moments in life like
stations to get off of. Told her where he'd gotten stuck and where
she shouldn't, saw eternity as the five seconds it takes to have a
sip of coffee from the cup that's already cold with the hopes that
somebody, if anybody, remembers you.

LETTER TO YOURSELF #4

Dear you,
You are twenty-five
holding lessons in your back pocket
that have left their burdens,
and the ghosts of your sins are coming to make claim
of what now seems like another life.
Surrounded by the unknown of what's to come by morning
when the crescendo lifts the curtain,
will I still find you there?
This weight feels old,
this story older,
the want to be put to rest somewhere.
Anywhere in fact,
if only for a moment
for a steady heartbeat
for a full breath.
The words are still in you
this journey is yours to make of it what you wish
no matter how long the silence may have reigned.
This voice reigns everlasting
remind yourself of that,
every day your reflection is not kind to itself.
By now, you've learned to love your parents anew
with all their own broken that they had hoped to hide forever
like any parent would.
Of a cruel world they do not wish us to be witness to,
for they will always see the child in you.
No matter how many lessons have been taught
and you,
the youth that they too once carried
with reckless conviction
the world at their fingertips.

IN THE SOUTHSIDE

In the southside of my father's heart
he is part man, part lost boy.
Carries all his regrets at the bottom of his feet
kept at bay, buried, muffled out, so it does not exist to him
and the mirror becomes easier to look at.
They don't keep him up at night he says
while he takes a sip,
the family portrait framed out,
this third ring doesn't fit as comfortably as the second
apparently, this ring didn't do the trick either.
He kept his promise,
went to his refuge across the ocean,
in between boyhood mountains,
and I miss the security of his closeness
being a phone call and drive away
and it is not that I need him.
He made sure of that
he, who taught it is better to do it by oneself, if one can,
and one will.
Always,
but there was comfort in knowing he could say "I am still here"
even in his silence.
For the moments a wise mind was needed.

In the southside of my mother's heart
she is still writing out what it means to be a woman
sins and all.
Whose reflection does not crack,
when they make less of her accent
whose will does not bend for fear of falling, of failing.
This is not to say that you haven't fallen
you've learned well what it takes to pick oneself up again
time after time.
Does not falter to the weight of her own life,
not all understand,

the baggage of having to piece together again
the broken mirage of a marriage for seventeen years
including her
including me.
If nothing else,
I ask for this resilience to find me whenever I need it most.
Not all will get the privilege,
to witness the survival from her own broken
her laughter,
a proclamation
that she has the audacity to smile
against everything that will ever try to drown her
and fail.

In the southside of the hearts that once loved me
holds a collection of alleyways of memories
and necessary lessons.
Somewhere I am collecting dust, in scattered pieces or whole.
I have stepped into hearts
the same way you put on a sweater
without planning it.
Not sure where I stand or if I stand at all
the ghost of me has probably been there
like the worn-out letter hidden in the drawer
maybe I'm stuffed in that corner closet
in a jacket pocket four years old, bent out of shape.
Who knows what my memory tastes like,
when they run it across their teeth from time to time
maybe she holds onto my ghost as briefly as a whisper
before the world peeks out to find her again.
Maybe I'm that skeleton that isn't talked about
as if to say,
it has been tucked out of existence there is nothing to see here.
Or maybe,
I am the story that will be remembered
when they talk about falling in love
I hope I do it justice if nothing else was done right.

In the southside of my own heart
I am rough around the edges,
always feeling more sinner than saint
tender hearted and bloody knuckled
with a tendency for recklessness.
I have loved in hopes that I do not fail at it like my parents did.
Learned the weight words carry in our own history
knowing the fine tune of a broken heart
leaves you a sharpened tongue,
with stories to tell to bellies full of wine.
But I still get afraid of liking my own silence for too long,
just like my father.
When she breaks your heart for the very last time
you will have learned how to bare your teeth and mean it.
Have a spine and stand in it,
when I do not know how to speak to God
which is often.
I am kept company by the whispers of memories
of when I've smiled and meant it.
An abundance of unfinished poems
words too many to know what to do with,
where to put them,
or who to give them to.
I pray they only cease when I can no longer put pen to paper
even then,
I will tell stories for the wind to carry until this body no longer exists.

In the southside
the truth comes out
bold, unforgiving
and oh how beautiful that is.

CPSIA information can be obtained
at www.ICGtesting.com
Printed in the USA
BVHW030918131020
590913BV00001B/100